30 New Worship Songs for all ages

"SING FOR JOY"

By
Graham & Margaret Millard

- ❖ SUITABLE FOR ALL AGES
- ❖ FOR FAMILY SERVICES
- ❖ FOR SCHOOL ASSEMBLIES
- ❖ SONGS FOR CHRISTIAN FESTIVALS AND SPECIAL OCCASIONS
- ❖ FULLY ILLUSTRATED
- ❖ BIBLICAL REFERENCES FOR EACH SONG
- ❖ SUGGESTIONS FOR CHILDREN'S ACTIONS
- ❖ THE WORDS OF SOME SONGS REPRODUCED AS OVERHEADS
- ❖ PERMISSION TO PHOTOCOPY ALL SONGS IF USED FOR EDUCATIONAL OR WORSHIP PURPOSES

PUBLISHED BY GRAHAM MILLARD – 2003

6, Waterside Lane
Sydling St. Nicholas
Dorchester
Dorset DT2 9NY

Tel & Fax 01300-341778
e-mail gmillard@fish.co.uk

ACKNOWLEDGEMENTS

Publishing this book has only been possible, thanks to considerable help from local friends. We would therefore like to place on record our thanks to:

★   Maggie Hooper and the children of class 2 of Thorner's C. of E. V.A. Primary School, Litton Cheney, Dorchester who enthusiastically tested out several of the songs.

★   Derek Robinson, a member of Dorset Christian Poetry Group, who has written a delightful selection of seasonal prayers ideal for inclusion in family services.

★   Charles and Penny Cordy who provided invaluable help while we learned to use the musical software and during the final editing stage. They also wrote the Winter's Carol which we have included.

★   Rev. Ken Scott (the Rector) and the Rev. Sue Chalk (Curate) of our local Benefice of Bradford Peverell, Stratton, Frampton and Sydling St.Nicholas for advice on biblical references.

★   Those who took the seasonal photographs in Sydling St.Nicholas, Malcolm Merrifield for Spring, Jonathan Alden, for Summer and Winter, and Catherine Bramble for Autumn.

★   Tim Stiles who checked out the guitar chords.

★   To Charminster School (near Dorchester) for advice on the composition of the School Song.

★   Richard Cropp who offered advice to resolve computer problems throughout the project.

★   Trevor and Alison Millard, who were pleased for us to include the song 'Let us celebrate your gift of love' composed especially for their marriage service.

★   Grandson Samuel for whom the Saucepan Song (No.7) was originally composed.

★   The following children in our village of Sydling St.Nicholas whose photographs we have included:-

    Kitty, Robert, and Suzanna Baird, Henry and William Dale, Catherine and Sophie Fowler, Alexander and Jessica Hallett, Katie, Olivia and George Hanson, Sabrina Lawrence and Joshua Stiles.

★   Creeds the Printers of Broadoak, Bridport, Dorset for their cooperation in printing the publication.

ISBN 0-9544511-0-4   ISMN M 9002078 0 7

FOREWORD

We hope this book of songs will be useful to meet a wide range of needs for family worship, school assemblies, Sunday Schools and Community Churches. The songs are all newly composed, although some have already been used at services within our benefice of Bradford Peverell, Stratton, Frampton and Sydling St.Nicholas.

Some of the songs are associated with Christian Festivals such as Easter, Harvest or Christmas. There is one song with words appropriate for a marriage service, another one suitable for an evening service and one (Join Hands Together) intended, rather like Auld Lang Syne, to be sung with the congregation holding hands in fellowship at the end of a service.

Some are composed especially for children, usually based on biblical stories; many of these provide opportunities for actions or the use of props. Those that are suitable for school assemblies have been tested out with the help of children at a local primary school: needless to say the children were quite forthcoming in suggesting improvements! Some of these songs find a way of linking everyday life (such as mobile phones!) with Christian messages.

Several of the family service songs simply remind us of fundamental truths, such as Constant Love (based on Psalm 51) or in song No. 2, the vastly different gifts each of us has been given to contribute during the course of our life. Biblical cross references are included for most of the songs.

Although the sequence generally follows a seasonal pattern, several songs equally could be well placed anywhere in the book. So there is no strict logic about the order: for example all songs suitable for school are not necessarily grouped together. Two pieces towards the end of the book, originally written as songs without words as a tribute to the passing of local villagers, are suitable for playing as voluntaries before or after a service.

For each season there is a selection of prayers set out in such a way that parents and children might like to share leading these within a family service. The words of a few of the songs for young children are reproduced in large print at the end of the book for use as overheads.

Photographs and drawings are included to remind us of the beautiful world we live in for which we can praise God through music, words and prayer.

Our joint efforts in providing this book were broadly divided by Margaret providing the photographs and illustrations and handling the word processing, and myself, composing the music and words. We thoroughly enjoyed doing it; we now hope many others will equally enjoy using the publication. The main objective has been to offer new songs that can be added to the existing musical repertoire for worship, but we also hope that through these songs some worshippers might gain new insights into their own Christian beliefs and values.

Graham and Margaret Millard   March 2003

INDEX

INDEX

1. CONSTANT LOVE

Con - stant love and all your mer - cy wash a - way my

sin; Take the e - vil that be - sets me,

make me clean with in

CONSTANT LOVE

(A song for forgiveness, based on the words of Psalm 51, verses 1 to 12.)

1. Constant love and all your mercy
   Wash away my sin;
   Take the evil that besets me,
   Make me clean within.

2. All my life I've sinned against you
   All my faults you know;
   Tho' you're right to judge my failings,
   Mercy, God please show.

3. Being sincere is what you ask for
   Cleanse my mind anew;
   Wash me, free me of all evil
   So that joy shines through.

4. Make me willing to obey you
   Help me make a start:
   Loving you in full repentance
   With a humble heart.

5. Create a pure heart through your spirit
   Do not banish me.
   Grant me joy of your salvation,
   I give myself to thee.

BIBLICAL REFERENCE

"Have mercy on me, O God
According to your unfailing love
According to your great compassion
Blot out all my transgressions
Wash away all my iniquity
And cleanse me from my sin."

Psalm 51. Verse 1.

---

2. THANK YOU FOR THE GIFTS

Oh Lord, Oh Lord, oh yes I love You so and thank you for the gifts which You be-stow; Oh Lord, Oh Lord, Oh yes I love you so, per-haps there are some which I do not yet know per-haps there are some which I do not yet know. Teach-ing or serv-ing with a

THANK YOU FOR THE GIFTS WHICH YOU BESTOW

Chorus   Oh Lord, oh Lord, oh yes I love you so,
And thank you for the gifts which you bestow;
Oh Lord, Oh Lord, Oh yes I love you so;
Perhaps there are some which I do not yet know;
Perhaps there are some which I do not yet know.

Verse 1   Teaching, or serving with a love that shows
Or offering others strength that grows;
Faithful living,
Mercy giving

          … for each of us there are some gifts God chose.

Repeat Chorus

Verse 2   Kindness and love which I may sometimes share
To ease a burden hard to bear;
Pain allaying,
Just by praying,

          … and letting people know I really care.

Repeat Chorus

Verse 3   Helping another Christian life to start,
Or words of knowledge to impart;
Sometimes leading or
Interceding,

          … or using simple gifts within my heart.

Repeat Chorus

BIBLICAL REFERENCES

1.   'We have different gifts… if a man's gift is serving, let him serve; if it is contributing to the needs of others, let him give generously; if it is leadership, let him govern diligently; if it is in showing mercy, let him do it cheerfully.'

                            (Romans 12. Verse 6 to 8.)

2.   'Open your homes to each other without complaining. Each one should use whatever gift he or she received to serve others.'

                            (1 Peter 4. Verse 9 to 10.)

3.   'But to each one of us grace has been given as Christ appointed it.'

                            (Ephesians 4. Verse 7.)

Picture opposite – Oilseed rape in full bloom in Sydling St. Nicholas

Spring

3. THE WORLD CAN BE BRIGHTER

BIBLICAL REFERENCE

"For God, who said 'Let light shine out of darkness', made his light shine in our hearts to give us the light of the knowledge of the glory of God in the face of Christ."

2 Corinthians. Chapter 4. Verse 6.

THE WORLD CAN BE BRIGHTER

Chorus

In this world there's great darkness,
But we all can bring light
Of such goodness and brightness,
To change wrong into right.

Chorus
(Repeated)

In this world there's great darkness,
But we all can bring light
Of such goodness and brightness,
To change wrong into right.

Verse 1.

It may just be small things
That each person can do;
But we may need each other
When one is too few.

Chorus

In this world there's great darkness,
But we all can bring light
Of such goodness and brightness,
To change wrong into right.

Verse 2.

So the world can be brighter:
If we try to do good
Such as loving our neighbours
As we know we all should.

Final Chorus

In this world there's great darkness,
But we all can bring light
Of such goodness and brightness,
To change wrong into right,
To change wrong into right.

EASTER AND SPRING FAMILY PRAYERS

Parent   Heavenly Father, who created all things and all seasons, we thank You for the beauty of spring. With Your hands You made the trees and the flowers to delight our eyes and to bring joy to our hearts.

Most of all, Father, we thank You that in this season, You gave Your only begotten son, our Lord, Jesus Christ, to die for us on the cross at Calvary, so that nothing will ever be able to separate us from Your love.

Amen.

Child   Lord we thank You for the lighter and warmer evenings that spring brings. We thank You for all the fun we have, playing in the fields and riding our bikes in the country lanes. We thank You for all the chocolate Easter eggs we get and for the painted ones we like to roll down the slopes.

Amen.

Child   Father we thank You for all the little lambs and chickens that we love to see in spring. And thank You for the lovely wild flowers we make into little posies to take home for our Mums, to show them we love them.

Amen.

Parent   Heavenly Father, we have much to be thankful for. Help us to make this a time of new beginnings, a time to cast off all those things that displease You, and a time to start our lives anew, safe in the knowledge of Your great forgiveness and redeeming love for us.

Amen.

4. JESUS DIED BUT NOT IN VAIN

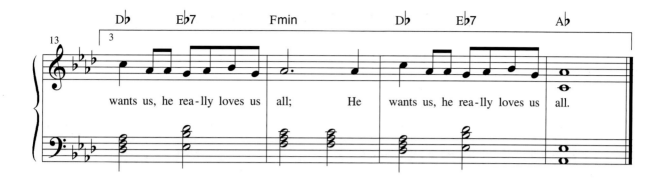

wants us, he rea-lly loves us all;   He wants us, he rea-lly loves us all.

JESUS DIED BUT NOT IN VAIN

1.   Jesus died, but not in vain,
For us he chose to bear the pain;
Three days his body lay
Until that Easter Day;
Then he rose,
Then he rose,
Jesus rose again.
So Jesus lives to save us all;
He asks us if it was worth it all?

2.   Jesus died, but not in vain,
For us he chose to bear the pain;
Three days his body lay
Until that Easter Day;
Then he rose,
Then he rose,
Jesus rose again.
So Jesus lives to save us all;
He asks us if we have heard his call?

3.   Jesus died, but not in vain,
For us he chose to bear the pain;
Three days his body lay
Until that Easter Day;
Then he rose,
Then he rose,
Jesus rose again.
So Jesus lives to save us all;
He wants us ... he really loves us all;

Slowly   He wants us, he really loves us all.

BIBLICAL REFERENCE

'For God so loved the world that he gave his only Son that whosoever believes in him shall not perish but have eternal life.'

John. Chapter 3. Verse 16.

---

5. EASTER JOY

Glory, Glory, Easter's Joy
For each girl and
ev - ery boy; The hea - vy stone has rolled a-way;
Hip, hip, hip, hoo - ray.

BIBLICAL REFERENCE

'Mary Magdalene, Mary the mother of Jesus, and Salome brought spices so that they might go to anoint Jesus' body ... just after sunrise they were on their way to the tomb and they asked each other "Who will roll the stone away from the entrance of the tomb?" But when they looked up, they saw that the stone, which was very large, had been rolled away.
As they entered the tomb, they saw a young man dressed in a white robe ... "Don't be afraid" he said, "you are looking for Jesus the Nazarene, who was crucified. He is not here. He has risen."

Mark Chapter 16. Extracts from Verses 1 to 6.

EASTER JOY

1.   Glory, glory Easter's Joy
             For each girl, and every boy;
             The heavy stone has rolled away,
             Hip, hip, hip hooray.

2.   Glory, glory Easter's Joy
             For each girl, and every boy;
             Now Christ has risen from the grave
             Everyone to save.

3.   Glory, glory Easter's Joy
             For each girl and every boy;
             The heavy stone has rolled away,
(Slower)   HIP – HIP – HIP - HOORAY.

PROPS AND ACTIONS

A black open umbrella or a large cardboard circular cut-out can be turned slowly to signify the stone being rolled away.

6. SOMEBODY'S KNOCKING AT MY DOOR

BIBLICAL REFERENCE

"Ask and it will be given to you;
Seek and you will find;
Knock and the door will be opened to you.
For everyone who asks receives;
He who seeks finds;
And to him who knocks, the door will be opened."

Matthew. Chapter 7. Verse 7.

SOMEBODY'S KNOCKING AT MY DOOR

Verse 1

Somebody's knocking at my door;
Should I go and let them in?
Somebody's knocking at my door;
Should I open up my sin?
Oh yes, I need you Lord
Oh yes, I need you Lord,
I want to give my life to you;
Oh yes, I need you Lord,
Oh yes, I need you Lord,
No one else but only you will do.

Verse 2

Jesus is knocking at my door;
I will go and let him in.
Jesus is knocking at my door;
To come and take away my sin.
Oh yes, I want you Lord
Oh yes, I want you Lord,
I want to give my life to you;
Oh yes, I want you Lord,
Oh yes, I want you Lord,
No one else but only you will do.

Verse 3

No more knocking at my door,
Jesus you have entered in.
No more knocking at my door,
You have washed away my sin.
So give your praise to God,
I give my praise to God;
For he has entered through my door.
So give your praise to God,
I give my praise to God,
I will have his love for evermore.

Final Chorus

No more knocking at my door,
No more knocking at my door,
Jesus has come in.

PROPS AND ACTIONS

**Small blocks of wood can be used to make
knocking noises to accompany
'knocking at the door' lines.**

7. LET'S PRAISE GOD UPON THE DRUM

LET'S PRAISE GOD UPON THE DRUM

1.	Let's praise God upon the drum;	BANG! BANG!
	He likes to know that you are having fun;	BANG! BANG!
	You might prefer to sing	
	Or play a tambourine,	
	Or if you haven't got one	
	You can simply bang a tin.	BANG!

2.	So you praise God with all that you have got;	BANG! BANG!
	It might be a jam jar or a pot;	BANG! BANG!
	You can sing or shout,	
	He knows you are about,	
	And he likes to know you love him such a lot,	BANG! BANG!
	And he likes to know you love him such a lot.	BANG! BANG!

Props – tambourine, jam jars, a tin, a pot, a drum, sticks and spoons

---

BIBLICAL REFERENCE

'Sing and make music in your hearts to the Lord, always giving thanks to God the Father for everything, in the name of our Lord Jesus Christ.'

Ephesians. Chapter 5. Verses 19 and 20.

Alternative words to sing when children are at home.

Props – Raid the kitchen for a frying pan, a selection of three saucepans and some wooden spoons.

THE SAUCEPAN SONG

1.	One big saucepan made the stew,	BANG! BANG! (Big saucepan)
	And another one was cooking too,	BANG! BANG! (Second saucepan)
	And the great big frying pan	
	Was heating up the oil	BANG! (Frying pan)
	And the tiny little saucepan,	
	It was coming to the boil.	BANG! (Little saucepan)

2.	So we all sat down to start to eat	BANG! BANG! (All pans)
	What we all thought would be a lovely treat;	BANG! BANG! (All pans)
	What we'd all forgot	
	To put in every pot,	
	Was the water that you have to heat,	BANG! BANG! (All pans)
	Was the water that you have to heat.	BANG! BANG! (All pans)

8. HELP ME TO KNOW

Help me to know there are ma-ny things to do, Help me to show that I love you;

Lord I need to pray to know your plan and then say Here I am. Show me the fut-ure be

yond the safe and known; help me to rea-lise that I am not a-lone; what is the chal-lenge what

plans are there for me? Some - where I'm need - ed that is a cert-ain-ty

HELP ME TO KNOW

• WORDS OF THIS SONG ON NEXT PAGE

BIBLICAL REFERENCES

'For I know the plans I have for you, declares the Lord,
plans to prosper you and not to harm you, plans to give you hope
and a future.'

Jeremiah. Chapter 29. Verse 11.

'I can do everything through Him who gives me strength.'

Philippians. Chapter 4. Verse 13.

'Everything is possible for him who believes.'

Mark. Chapter 9. Verse 23.

HELP ME TO KNOW THERE ARE MANY THINGS TO DO

Chorus   Help me to know there are many things to do,
Help me to show that I love you;
Lord I need to pray to know your plan,
And then say " Here I am."

Verse 1   Show me the future beyond the safe and known;
Help me to realise that I am not alone;
What is the challenge? What plans are there for me?
Somewhere I'm needed; that is a certainty.

Chorus   Help me to know there are many things to do,
Help me to show that I love you;
Lord I need to pray to know your plan,
And then say "Here I am."

Verse 2   Help me to serve you perhaps in pastures new,
Or try some new tasks I thought I couldn't do;
I know you want me, your call is always clear,
Now I should heed it, there is no need to fear.

Chorus   Help me to know there are many things to do,
Help me to show that I love you;
Lord I need to pray to know your plan,
And then say "Here I am."

Verse 3   I really need you to guide my way ahead;
'All things are possible', that's what the Bible said;
I know that 'cannot' could surely change to 'can,'
With you to help me, I'm important in your plan.

Chorus   Help me to know there are many things to do,
Help me to show that I love you;
Lord I need to pray to know your plan,
And then say "Here I am."

Picture opposite – The footbridge at Ham Farm, Sydling St.Nicholas

Summer

9. OUR SCHOOL SONG

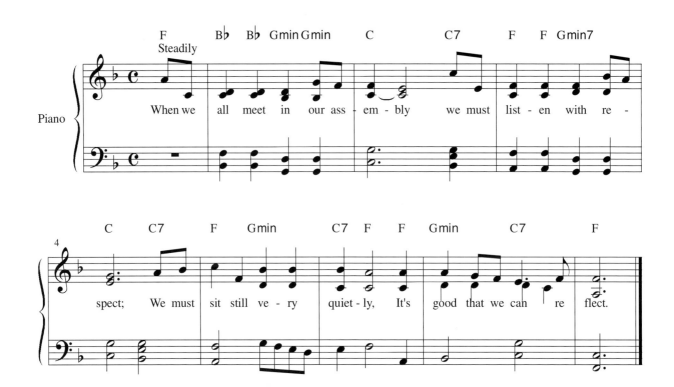

Children of Thorner's Church of England VA Primary School, Litton Cheney, in celebration mood!

OUR SCHOOL SONG

1.   When we all meet in our assembly
   We must listen with respect;
   We must sit still very quietly,
   It's good that we can reflect.

2.   When we're sitting in the classroom
   Learning things or taking tests;
   We must all work very quietly,
   And always do our best.

3.   When we're outside in the playground,
   When we're running everywhere,
   To our friends we must be kindly
   And take lots of extra care.

4.   As we move about the building
   Be polite to those we pass,
   Do not run or be too noisy
   As we go back to class.

5.   We must listen to our teachers
   'Cos they want us to succeed;
   And we must be very helpful
   To those who have special needs.

6.   If we do these things together
   We will have a happy school;
   And we must love one another,
   As Jesus loves us all.

Alternative last verse

         All these things are written for us
In the code we have at school
And we must love one another
As Jesus loves us all.

10. WHEN I TURN TO YOU LORD

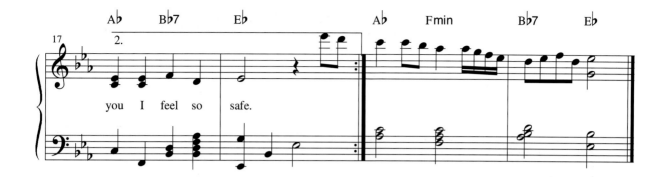

WHEN I TURN TO YOU LORD

When I turn to you Lord,
Past sins soon disappear;
And when I turn to you Lord,
I lose all sense of fear.
And when I turn to you Lord,
I wonder at your grace;
For when I turn to you Lord,
With you I feel so safe.
And when I turn to you Lord,
I wonder at your grace;
For when I turn to you Lord,
With you I feel so safe.

BIBLICAL REFERENCES

'Repent then, and turn to God, so that your sins
may be wiped out, that times of refreshing may
come from the Lord.'

Acts. Chapter 3. Verse 19.

'Come unto me, all ye that labour and are heavy
laden, and I will give you rest.'

Matthew. Chapter 11. Verse 28.

---

11. JESUS WE THANK YOU WITH JOY IN OUR HEARTS

JESUS WE THANK YOU WITH JOY IN OUR HEARTS

First   Jesus we thank you with joy in our hearts
Chorus For your wonderful world;
        Jesus we all want to sing and then dance
        In your wonderful world:
        Mountain streams and rainbow beams
        And verdant greenery,
        Make wondrous scenery,
        Creatures lying,
        Birds they are a-flying
        And you might just hear
           the buzzing of the bee.

First   O what a world,
Verse   What seas, what land,
        And the forests and the flowers and the fell;
        O what a world
        You've beautifully planned
        Where you brought us here to dwell.

Second Jesus we thank you with joy in our hearts
Chorus For your wonderful world;
        Jesus we all want to sing and then dance
        In your wonderful world:
        Sea and sky, the moon on high
        Reveals your majesty,
        No distance we can see;
        The wind is blowing,
        The mighty tide is flowing
        And you might just feel some spraying
           from the sea.

2nd   O what a world
Verse   Both here and abroad,
        We marvel at all that we see.
        O what a world,
        Where we're close to our Lord
        And that's where our love should be.

Final   Jesus we thank you with joy in our hearts
Chorus For your wonderful world;
        Jesus we all want to sing and then dance
        In your wonderful world:
        Scents and sounds and shapes abound
        In vast variety,
        To smell and hear and see,
        You're inspiring,
        We just keep admiring
        As we sing and raise our song of joy to thee.

SEASONAL PRAYERS

Here in the folds of gentle hills,
The swathes of golden daffodils,
And mothers pointing out the lambs
To gurgling babies in their prams.
And in the meadows drawing cowslip,
Town youngsters on a nature trip.
A thousand signs upon the earth,
Proclaim the wonders of new birth.

Thank You Lord for spring.

*****

Sunny days beside the sea,
That's the place I like to be.
Mum prefers to spend the hours
Tending to her garden flowers.
Dad's content to read his books
Down by the stream, with baby ducks.
Sister thinks it's very cool
To pose beside the swimming pool.

Thank You Lord for summer.

*****

Piled high trailers in the lane
Tells us harvest's here again.
Soon the crops are neatly stored,
Provisions from our gracious Lord.
Golden leaves fall from the trees
And gently flutter in the breeze.
And having given of their best,
Earth and man have earned their rest.

Thank You Lord for autumn.

*****

Frozen pond beside the mill,
Robin on the window sill.
Berried holly in the hedges,
Happy kids on home-made sledges.
Peals of bells across the earth,
Remind us of our Saviour's birth.
In this season, one year ends
And our Lord, another sends.

Thank You Lord for winter.'

12. WHAT A GREAT GOAL

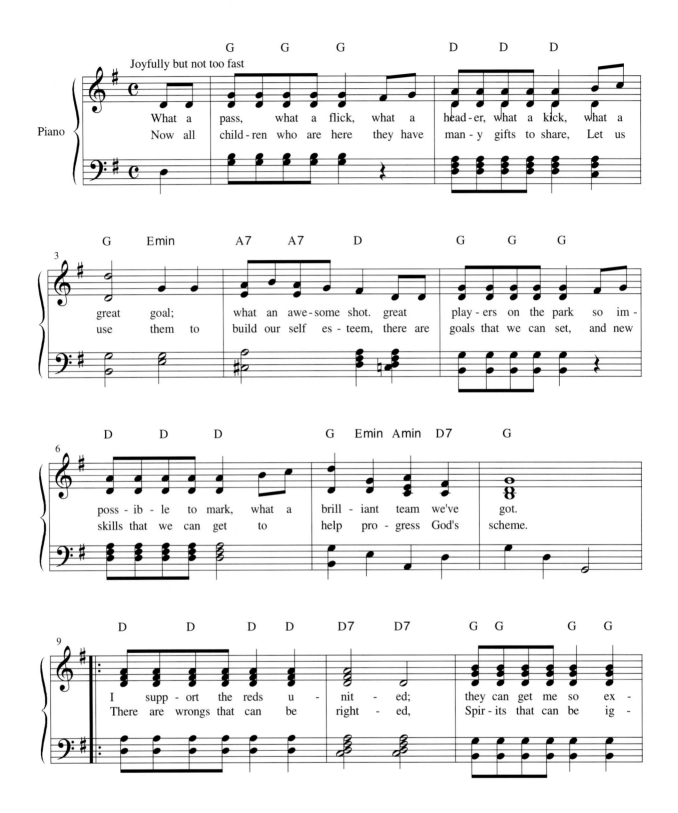

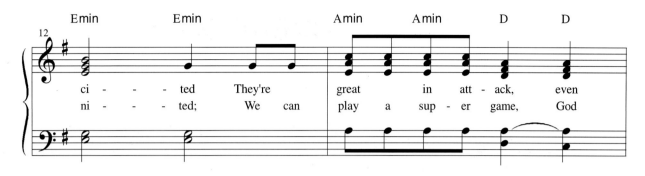

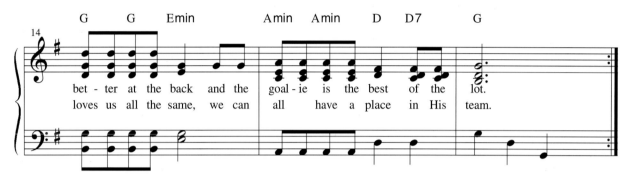

WHAT A GREAT GOAL

1. What a pass, what a flick,
What a header, what a kick,
What a great goal; what an awesome shot.
Great players on the park
So impossible to mark,
What a brilliant team we've got.

I support the reds united;
They can get me so excited;
They're great in attack,
Even better at the back,
And the goalie is the best of the lot.

Repeat ..... I support the reds .....

2. Now all children who are here
They have many gifts to share,
Let us use them to build our self esteem,
There are goals that we can set,
And new skills that we can get
To help progress God's scheme.

There are wrongs that can be righted,
Spirits that can be ignited;
We can play a super game,
God loves us all the same,
We can all have a place in His team.

Repeat ..... There are wrongs .....

BIBLICAL REFERENCE – HOME OR AWAY

'So we make it our goal to please Him whether we are AT HOME in the body or AWAY from it.'
2 Corinthians. Chapter 5. Verse 9.

---

13. CLEANSE MY SOUL

BIBLICAL REFERENCES

This song is derived from Biblical references concerning a range of human worries, including:–

Verse 1 **Isaiah. Chapter 54. Verse 4.**
'Do not be afraid; you will not suffer shame, do not fear disgrace.'

Verse 2 **Luke. Chapter 12. Verse 22.**
'Do not worry about your life, what you will eat, or about your body, what you will wear.
Who of you by worrying can add a single hour to your life?'

Luke. Chapter 12. Verse 32.
'Your heart will always be where your riches are.'

Verse 3 **1 Peter. Chapter 3. Verses 13 and 14.**
'Who is going to harm you if you are eager to do good?
Even if you suffer for what is right, you are blessed.'

Verse 4 **Proverbs. Chapter 3. Verse 25.**
'Have no fear of sudden disaster or of the ruin that overtakes the wicked.'

Jeremiah. Chapter 29. Verse 11.
'For I know the plans I have for you, plans to prosper you and not to harm you,
plans to give you hope and a future.'

CLEANSE MY SOUL

Chorus   Cleanse my soul and make me whole,
Remove anxiety.
Purge those fears, I've held for years,
So now renewed I'll live for thee.

Verse 1.   We should not hold
Deep rooted feelings
Of hate, or fear
To ever last;
For shame or anger
God gives his healing;
Our minds can rest now,
What's gone, has passed.

Chorus   Cleanse my soul.......

Verse 2.   We should not yearn
For more possessions,
Should we not be
Well satisfied?
Our hearts hold riches,
We all have blessings,
Save these for heaven,
God does provide.

Chorus   Cleanse my soul.......

Verse 3.   Do what is good
Be strong and true,
Happy you'll be
For doing right.
There might be hardship
And perils for you,
Fear not, nor worry,
You're in God's sight.

Chorus   Cleanse my soul.......

Verse 4.   Dismiss your cares
About tomorrow,
Imagined dangers
Do not fear.
There will be more joy
And sometimes sorrow;
God has his own plan,
He's always near.

Chorus   Cleanse my soul........

SUMMER FAMILY PRAYERS

Parent   Heavenly Father, who provides for all our needs throughout the year, we thank You for the season of summer. We thank You for the sunshine that warms the land and works together with the light refreshing rain to bring forth the crops and the fruit on which we depend. We thank You for the many pleasures we enjoy during this season: for the times spent in the countryside or by the sea; enjoying outdoor pursuits or just relaxing in our gardens or parks. For all these things, Father, we humbly offer You our thanks and praise.
Amen.

Child   Lord, we thank You for all the fun that summer brings: playing games, rambling in the countryside or swimming in the sea and the rivers. We thank You for our holidays, spent with our parents, relations or friends, and for the adventures we share with our friends at summer camps run by schools and youth organisations.
Amen.

Child   Father, we thank You for the lovely flowers and berries we see in the countryside and in the parks during summertime and for the picnics we like to have on the grassy banks of a stream or in the shade of a mighty tree. We thank You for all the birds and insects we see on our walks and for the lovely warmth of the sun on our faces and for the cool breezes when it gets hot.
Amen.

Parent   Heavenly Father, help us never to take for granted the wonderful gifts that You so graciously provide for us; not least of those gifts: the four seasons, of which summer is but one. As we play or toil throughout this summer, help us always to see the workings of Your hand in all the beauty and the richness that surrounds us, and make us truly thankful.
Amen.

14. MOSES' SONG

MOSES' SONG

1. The King of Egypt made a law
Affecting every town;
New baby boys of Israelites
Would die, they'd have to drown.

2. But Jochebed who loved her son,
She could not bear the thought;
She put him in a basket
So he could not be caught.

3. This floated in the rushes
Along the River Nile,
And Miriam, his sister,
Kept watch for quite a while.

4. One day a princess came along
And found his hiding place;
She picked him up and cuddled him,
A smile came to his face.

5. So Miriam ran home to Mum,
The princess had agreed
That Jochebed could have her son
Back home to nurse and feed.

6. But when he grew much older,
The palace was his home;
The princess she had wanted him
To be her very own.

7. He grew up to be Moses,
A wise man, who one day
Would lead his people from that land
To a country far away.

BIBLICAL REFERENCE   Exodus. Chapter 2. Verses 1 to 10.

15. ONCE UPON A SUNNY DAY

Once up-on a sun-ny day, id-eal to have a break; Jes-us and his friends, they thought they'd sail a-cross the lake. The sea was blue and ver-y calm, the sky was at its best; so Jes-us thought he'd take this chance to lie down for a rest.

ONCE UPON A SUNNY DAY

1.   Once upon a sunny day,
Ideal to have a break;
Jesus and his friends, they thought
They'd sail across the lake.

The sea was blue and very calm,
The sky was at its best;
So Jesus thought he'd take this chance
To lie down for a rest.

2.   Suddenly the wind got up,
It blew and blew and blew.
The friends of Jesus all got scared
And wondered what to do.

The boat it tossed and turned about,
There was no time to think;
The water started rushing in,
The boat began to sink.

3.   Then they woke up Jesus
They thought they might all drown;
Jesus shouted out "BE STILL,"
At once the wind died down.

Then Jesus gave his friends this pledge
That still today is true;
That if you always trust in God,
He'll always care for you.

BIBLICAL REFERENCE

Mark. Chapter 4. Verses 35 to 41. The story of Jesus calming the storm.

---

16. LET US CELEBRATE YOUR GIFT OF LOVE

LET US CELEBRATE YOUR GIFT OF LOVE

(A song for a marriage service)

Verse 1   Love for the bride and bridegroom

Come join them in love,
And bless this very special day.
Come join them with love, and
Guide them through their lives' uncertain way;
May the vows which they make now as they join their hands,
May they stay and help them both in every circumstance,
Oh Lord we want to pray
That they'll be blessed today,
Let us celebrate their day of love;
O Lord we want to pray
That they'll be blessed today,
Let us celebrate their day of love;
Let us celebrate their day of love.

Verse 2. Love for the World

If there was more love
Where caring and sharing prevailed,
If there was more love
And Jesus our Saviour was hailed;
Then such joys of today could be in every place
And the problems of the world would be less hard to face,
O let us pray your Word
It can be spread and heard,
Let us celebrate your Word of love;
O let us pray your Word
It can be spread and heard,
Let us celebrate your Word of love,
Let us celebrate your Word of love.

Verse 3. Love for us all

Come bless us with love
And renew the vows we too have made;
Come bless us with love
And forgive us our sins for which you've paid;
For you died on the Cross so you would save us all,
Gave us faith and hope and love when we might start to fall,
O Lord we want to pray
We will be blessed today,
Let us celebrate your Gift of love;
O Lord we want to pray
We will be blessed today,
Let us celebrate your Gift of love,
Let us celebrate your Gift of love.

Picture opposite – View from Cerne Hill beechwood towards UpSydling, Dorset.

Autumn

17. DAVID AND GOLIATH

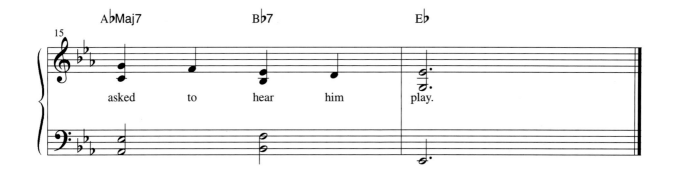

asked   to   hear   him   play.

DAVID AND GOLIATH

1.   Young David was a shepherd boy,
    Lived on his father's farm.
    He had to fight off grizzly bears
    To save his sheep from harm.

    He taught himself to play the harp,
    He practised every day.
    King Saul was told how good he was,
    So asked to hear him play.

2.   Now things were getting dangerous
    For all the Israelites;
    Their neighbours who were Philistines
    Were spoiling for a fight.

    They had a massive army,
    Goliath was in charge,
    Both strong and sly, and twelve foot high,
    Yes, he was very large.

Verses 3 to 5 continued on next page

BIBLICAL REFERENCE

For the full story read:–

1 Samuel. Chapter 16. Verses 14 to 23, and Chapter 17. Verses 1 to 54.

DAVID AND GOLIATH (continued)

3.   Goliath strutted up and down,
He laughed, he jeered, he roared;
He clattered in his armour plate,
And swished his mighty sword.

So who would fight this giant man?
Saul wondered what to do.
Then David boldly told the king:
"I'll kill him off for you."

4.   So David tried some armour on,
Too big, it didn't fit.
He couldn't use his arms or legs,
Nor could he stand or sit.

But David had a better plan;
He'd fight him with his sling;
He knew that if he prayed to God
He reckoned he could win.

5.   He swung his sling, a stone flew fast
Towards Goliath's head;
The giant screamed, crashed to the ground,
One hit – and he was dead.

The Philistines then fled away,
Saul's daughter David wed;
And when the king grew old and died,
Young David ruled instead.

HARVEST AND AUTUMN FAMILY PRAYERS

Parent   Father in Heaven, who created every season, and a time for every matter under heaven, we give You our thanks for the season of autumn in which we are richly blessed with the harvest from the land and the beauty of the countryside.
The leaves on the trees turn from green to burnished gold and the scented smell of log fires brings back memories of other autumns long gone. For the food that nourishes our bodies and the sights and smells that gladden our souls, we offer You our thanks and praise.
Amen.

Child   Lord, thank You for Harvest-time when we can sit on a fence and watch the combine-harvesters collecting in the crops from the fields. We like autumn, Lord, because all the leaves fall from the trees and go all crispy and make a lovely rustling noise when we kick through the piles of them in the lane. Also, we can collect conkers and have contests with our friends. Thank You for autumn, Lord. Amen.

Child   We like autumn, Lord, because this is when we go into the garden with the adults and help rake up all the dead leaves and have a bonfire which has a lovely smell. Sometimes we are allowed to buy some roasted chestnuts from a man in the town who has a sort of barrow with a fire in it. Thank You for autumn, Lord. Amen.

Parent   Heavenly Father, there is no end to the great goodness that You bestow on each and every one of us. Help us never to take for granted the wonders of the autumn season: the harvests You so graciously provide and the breathtaking beauty of the earth You created for us.
Amen.

18. HARVEST TIME IS HERE AGAIN

HARVEST TIME IS HERE AGAIN

**(Ideal for a Harvest Festival service –
Verse 2 provides opportunities to use a few visual aids)**

Chorus   Harvest time is here again,
Every season God has planned;
We thank Him for the sun and rain,
And the goodness of the land.

Verse 1   We give thanks to all those
Who make us nice clothes,
And all those who farm our crops,
And fishermen too, and many folk who...
Serve in our local shops.

Chorus   Harvest time is here again,
Every season God has planned;
We thank Him for the sun and rain,
And the goodness of the land.

Verse 2   Some sugar and tea,
And macaroni,
Some marmalade and some jam,
A tin of rice pud*
Always tastes good,*
And a great big tin of ham.

Chorus   Harvest time is here again,
Every season God has planned;
We thank Him for the sun and rain,
And the goodness of the land.

3rd Verse continued on next page

Alternative lines can be :-

*   'A tin of creamed rice
Always tastes nice'

Verse 3   The gifts we bring here,
            Will soon bring some cheer
            To people elsewhere in need,
            Who have little to eat,
            Let alone get a treat,
(slower)   Let's send these gifts God speed.

Final Chorus Harvest time is here again,
              Every season God has planned;
              We thank him for the sun and rain
              And the goodness of ....
              And the goodness of ....
              And the goodness of ....
              And the goodness of the land.

BIBLICAL REFERENCE

'Then God said, "Let the land produce vegetables:
seed-bearing plants and trees on the land that bear
fruit with seed in it, according to their various kinds."
And it was so...... and God saw that it was good.'

Genesis Chapter 1. Verses 11 and 12.

---

19. GOD LOVES A NICE CUP OF TEA

GOD LOVES A NICE CUP OF TEA

God made rhubarb, God made me,
God made apples to grow upon a tree,
God made cheese and a stick of celery,
And God made a lovely cup of tea,
And God made a lovely cup of tea.

God made beans, see how they run,
God made rain, the stars and sun,
God made tears and God made fun,
And God made a pot of tea for one,
And God made a pot of tea for one.

God loves you and God loves me,
Everywhere his love you see,
Don't forget – quite possibly,
That God loves a nice cup of tea,
That God loves a nice cup of tea,
(Slower)
THAT GOD LOVES A NICE CUP OF TEA – CHA – CHA – CHAR.

*   A young children's hymn.
*   Actions can be introduced as an option with teapots or cups and saucers.
*   Additionally sticks of rhubarb, apples, sticks of celery, cheese, runner beans, pictures of stars and the sun can be held up by individual children.

BIBLICAL REFERENCE

"For by him all things were created;
things in heaven and on earth,
visible and invisible."

Colossians. Chapter 1. Verse 16.

20. TIME TO GIVE, TO LOVE AND TO PRAISE

(A HARVEST SONG)

TIME TO GIVE, TO LOVE AND TO PRAISE

Verse 1   Harvest time is a time to send
           Wanted gifts we all can afford;
           Broken lives these may usefully mend
           In poorer lands abroad:
           These broken lives need mending,
           Our prayer to God we raise:

Chorus   Harvest time, harvest time
           Time to give,
           To love, and to praise.

Verse 2   Harvest time is a time to think
           Of a world where much more could be shared;
           So many lack cleaner water to drink,
           So money for that could be spared;
           For this there should be more spending,
           Our prayers to God we raise:

Chorus   Harvest time, harvest time
           Time to give,
           To love, and to praise.

Verse 3   Harvest time reminds us all
           Of the seeds of the love Jesus sowed;
           Mercies to us are so wonderful,
           His gifts to us all bestowed;
           His love is never ending,
           Our prayer to God we raise:

Chorus   Harvest time, harvest time
           Time to give,
           To love, and to praise.

BIBLICAL REFERENCE

'Remember this; whoever sows sparingly will also reap sparingly, and whoever sows generously will also reap generously. Each man should give what he has decided in his heart to give, not reluctantly or under compulsion, for God loves a cheerful giver.'

2 Corinthians. Chapter 9. Verses 6 and 7.

21. BURRHH, BURRHH
MY MOBILE PHONE

BURRHH, BURRHH, MY MOBILE PHONE

1. *Burrhh – Burrhh*, my mobile phone,
I - expect I've left the thing at home.
Never mind; God speaks to me
Anytime no rent, no fee.
Anytime no rent, no fee.

2. Hear - this, do not forget,
Hear this message through the internet.
www dot back slash com.
Jesus loves us – all day long,
Jesus loves us - all day long.

Quieter.Slower
Very quiet and
Very slow

3. At home, at school, Jesus connects
Not – by phone, or E-mail or by text.
Sshh, sshh, sshh, there is no sound,
Everywhere Jesus is around,
Everywhere Jesus is around.

Louder

4. *Burrhh – Burrhh*, receive that call,
It's from Jesus Christ who loves us all;
Don't hang up, please don't do that;
Slow   He will listen, he loves to have a chat,
He will listen, he loves to have a chat;

Very Very Loud   *Burrhh – Burrhh – MY MOBILE PHONE.*

TEMPO AND ACTIONS

This song needs to be sung quite slowly in order to fit in the words.

Throughout Verses 1 to 4   **Hold phone as if using it.**

Last line of Verse 4   **Hold phone high above head and shout out the lines.**

PROPS

All children could have cardboard cutouts of a phone in different colours or make phones using multilink or unifix pieces, as in the picture below.

**Class 2 of Thorner's Church of England VA Primary School, Litton Cheney
all busy on their phones!**

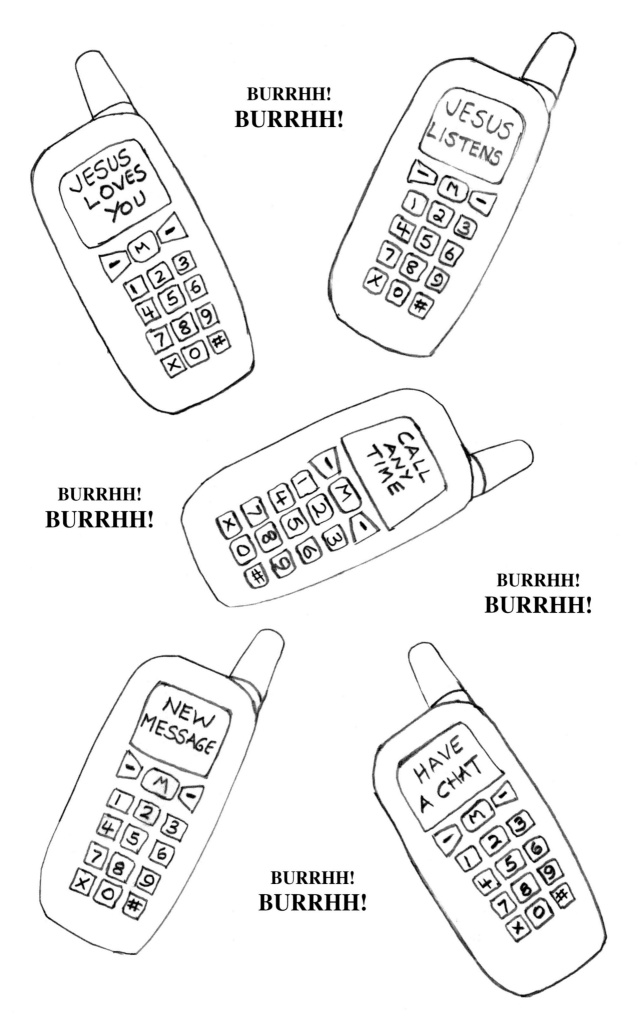

22. LORD REFRESH ME
(AN EVENING SONG)

Lord re-fresh me, Lord please bless me as my day un-winds; I must pause to praise and thank you as I rest my soul and mind. Spare me from those night time fears which strike in man-y ways; in

BIBLICAL REFERENCES

'Cast all your anxiety on him because he cares for you.'

1 Peter. Chapter 5. Verse 7.

'And the Lord of all grace will restore you and make you strong, firm and steadfast.'

1 Peter. Chapter 5. Verse 10.

'He leads me beside quiet waters
He restores my soul.'

Psalm 23. Verses 2-3.

'He who refreshes others will himself be refreshed.'

Proverbs 1. Verse 25.

LORD REFRESH ME

Verse 1   Lord refresh me,
Lord please bless me
As my day unwinds;
I must pause to pray and thank you
As I rest my soul and mind.

Chorus   Spare me from
Those night time fears
Which strike in many ways;
Increasing faith will help me wake,
My life restored,
To serve you Lord,
And live a better day.
My life restored,
To serve you Lord,
And live a better day.

Verse 2   Lord each evening,
Before sleeping
I should talk with you,
Then next morning, new strength dawning,
I'll be clearer what to do.

Chorus – Repeat

CHRISTMAS AND WINTER FAMILY PRAYERS

Parent   Heavenly Father, who made all things, we thank You for the season of winter. We thank You for the beauty of the winter landscape when the leafless trees display the intricacy of their design, and animals and men leave the evidence of their passing in the footprints in the snow. Lord of heaven, who gives us all we need in due season, we thank You that You chose this season to give us the most precious gift of all: Your Son, our saviour, Jesus Christ, to be with us throughout every day, of every season, for ever more.
Amen.

Child   Lord, we thank You for winter and all the fun we have in the snow with our sledges; and when we go skating on the frozen ponds in the park. We thank You for all the warm clothing we have when we are outside and for the hot meals and drinks that are waiting for us when we get home.
Amen.

Child   Father in heaven, we thank You for the winter season. We thank You for Christmas-time when we go round the houses with our lanterns, carol singing, and later eating hot mince pies in front of crackling log fires. We thank You for the fun we have building a snowman and dressing it up with Dad's old hat and Grandad's old pipe stuck in its mouth. Most of all, Lord, we thank You for sending baby Jesus to us, so that when he grew up He would teach us what is right.
Amen.

Parent   Heavenly Father, how abundant is Your goodness to Your people. Help us never to take for granted the wonders of Your creation. We give You praise for the four seasons and for the moon You made to mark them. In the present season of winter, help us to see and rejoice in all that is good and beautiful in it and bless your Holy name.
Amen.

23. MR WISE AND MR FOOLISH

MR WISE AND MR FOOLISH

1.
Mr Wise he built a house,
He built it on a rock.
He dug and dug, and worked so hard,
He worked right round the clock.

Then finally the job was done,
The house was built to last;
And when the wind and rain lashed down,
The house stood firm and fast.

2.
Mr Foolish built his house,
Some sandy soil he found;
The house was very quickly built
On very shallow ground.

He hadn't lived there very long,
One night he was asleep;
A storm blew up and knocked it down,
It tumbled in a heap.

3.
Down it fell because we know
His house was badly planned;
Mr Foolish should have known
His house would never stand.

The moral of this story,
It is easy now to tell;
So when you have a job to do (pause)
Have faith and do it well.

> **BIBLICAL REFERENCE**
>
> **Matthew Chapter 7. Verses 24 to 27.**

24. THERE'S A SPRING IN MY STEP

THERE'S A SPRING IN MY STEP

Verse 1

There's a spring in my step when I walk with my Lord,
What a power, what a King, what a friend;
Many things I can share with my Lord in a prayer,
It's a time I look forward to spend.

Chorus

Oh what a friend, Oh what a power,
Oh what a strength, and such love;
He will listen and chat
About this, about that
Such as problems that have to be solved.
I can call any time, he is always on line,
And He loves to get really involved.

Verse 2

There's a spring in my step, as I live out my life
With Jesus nearby at my side;
I can trust in my friend, from beginning to end,
He's my Redeemer, my Saviour, my Guide.

Final Chorus

Oh what a friend, Oh what a power,
Oh what a strength and such love;
He will listen and chat
About this, about that
Such as problems that have to be solved.
I can call any time, he is always on line,
And He loves to get really involved.
Oh what a friend, always in touch
Thank you my Jesus, I love you so much.

BIBLICAL REFERENCES

'Whether you turn to the right or to the left, your ears will hear a voice behind you, saying, "this is the way; walk in it."

Isaiah Chapter 30. Verse 21.

'Never will I leave you; never will I forsake you.'

Hebrews Chapter 13. Verse 5.

Picture opposite - Snow covered view of Sydling St.Nicholas looking west towards Cowdown Hill

Winter

25. A WINTER'S CAROL

Penny and Charles Cordy

A WINTER'S CAROL

Verse 1   In Bethlehem town on a cold winter's night
           A star shone up high overhead.
           In a stable so bare Mary cradled her child
           In a manger with straw for his bed.

Verse 2   Close by in the fields shepherds watched o'er their sheep
           As angels appeared in the night,
           With a message of hope for the world down below
           God's own son born to give us his light.

Verse 3   Then the shepherds they hastened with joy in their hearts,
           To the stable where Jesus was born,
           And the world celebrates every year at this time
           Christ's own birthday on Christmas morn.

Sunday School Nativity Scene at Sydling St.Nicholas Church

BIBLICAL REFERENCE

'And Mary gave birth to her first born, a son. She wrapped him in cloths and placed him in a
manger, because there was no room for them in the inn.
And there were shepherds living out in the fields nearby, keeping watch over their flocks by
night. An angel of the Lord appeared to them, and the glory of the Lord shone around them.'

Luke. Chapter 2. Verses 7 to 9.

---

26. COME AND WORSHIP

(A CHRISTMAS SONG)

an - gel voi - ces prais - ing, wise men were travell - ing far,

Watch - ing that shin - ing star to see the new born King.

BIBLICAL REFERENCE

'The angel said to them, "Do not be afraid, I bring you good news of great joy that will be for all people. Today in the town of David a Saviour has been born to you. He is Christ the Lord. This will be a sign to you, you will find the baby wrapped in cloths and lying in a manger." Suddenly a great company of the heavenly host appeared with the angel, praising God and saying,

"Glory to God in the highest,
And on earth peace to men."

Luke. Chapter 2. Verses 10-14.

COME AND WORSHIP

1.
Come and worship,
Come and worship,
Let's proclaim our Saviour's birth;
Come and worship,
Come and worship,
Jesus came to us on earth.

To a world so lost in sin,
Jesus gently entered in,
Flocks of sheep were lazing,
Angel voices praising,
Wise men were travelling far,
Watching that shining star
To see the new born King.

2.
Come and worship,
Come and worship,
May this Christmas time bring joy;
Come and worship,
Come and worship,
Let us praise this baby boy.

May the Christmas stockings fill
A troubled world with more goodwill;
May more love prevailing
Overcome its failings,
O may this Christmas song
Reach out to those who long
For love that you instill.

3.
Alleluya,
Alleluya,
Christmas is a time for praise;
Alleluya,
Alleluya,
Voices unto Jesus raise.

Joseph, Mary and you alone
In that manger as your home;
What a life you started,
What great love imparted;
Oh what great joy you bring,
We worship you as King,
"It's Christmas" – let's all sing.

A PRAYER FOR CHRISTMAS

Heavenly Father, thank You for Christmas;
    for sending Your son into the world
    to save sinners
    like me.
Thank You for the moment of his coming:
    a baby
    born in a stable,
    wrapped in strips of cloth,
    His bed, an animal's eating trough;
    and yet, amidst that humble setting,
    loved
    and worshipped
    and adored,
    by lowly, simple men,
    shepherds,
    who had nothing to bring but themselves,
    and by wise rich men,
    bearing gifts of gold, frankincense and myrrh.
Surely, Your sign to us Father:
    that those who believe in the name of the Lord Jesus Christ
    and follow His commands,
    whether they be poor or lowly in status,
    or blessed with wisdom and earthly wealth,
    can find acceptance in Your sight,
    if, just as they are,
    they come.

27. JOIN HANDS TOGETHER

HOW THIS SONG CAN BE USED

The party piece 'Auld Lang Syne' provided the idea for this song. Just as that song brings everybody together to celebrate the end of a party, this song 'Join Hands Together' can provide a joyful end to a family service, proclaiming our faith and uniting the congregation in fellowship.

If the design of the church (or church hall) makes it possible, the congregation can join hands and sing this song, even in a circle if it is practicable to do so.

The picture overleaf shows this happening at a service in Stratton, Dorset. It's a great way to return home and start a new week.

JOIN HANDS TOGETHER

Verse 1   Join hands together,
Praise him for ever,
We worship you above;
Help one another,
As sister and brother,
We want to share our love.
Our faith proclaim,
Rejoice in your name,
But help us on our way;
It's hard for me,
To always be (pause)
What you expect each day.

Verse 2   As we depart,
New strength in our heart
You answer our every call;
At work and home,
We want to make known,
That Jesus died for us all.
Our faith proclaim,
Rejoice in your name,
Unite us as we go;
Whatever the task,
Of us you ask (pause)
Our faith we have to show.

Final Chorus Join hands together,
Praise him for ever,
(Quietly)   Jesus died for us all;
Jesus died for us all;
(Forte)   JE – SUS – AROSE
For us all.

Part of the congregation singing this at the end of a Family Service at Stratton, Dorset

28. SYDLING SONG WITHOUT WORDS
(IN MEMORY OF MURIEL SYMES)

Slowly with feeling

29. SYDLING SONG WITHOUT WORDS

(IN MEMORY OF FRED WELLSPRING)

OVERHEAD WORDS FOR MOSES' SONG (14)

1. The King of Egypt made a law
    affecting every town;
    New baby boys of Israelites
    Would die, they'd have to drown.

2. But Jochebed who loved her son,
    She could not bear the thought;
    She put him in a basket
    So he could not be caught.

3. This floated in the rushes
    Along the River Nile,
    And Miriam, his sister,
    Kept watch for quite a while.

4. One day a princess came along
    And found his hiding place;
    She picked him up and cuddled him,
    A smile came to his face.

5. So Miriam ran home to Mum,
    The princess had agreed
    That Jochebed could have her son
    Back home to nurse and feed.

6. But when he grew much older,
    The palace was his home;
    The princess she had wanted him
    To be her very own.

7. He grew up to be Moses,
    A wise man, who one day
    Would lead his people from that land
    To a country far away.

OVERHEAD WORDS FOR
ONCE UPON A SUNNY DAY (15)

1.   Once upon a sunny day,
Ideal to have a break;
Jesus and his friends, they thought
They'd sail across the lake.

The sea was blue and very calm,
The sky was at its best;
So Jesus thought he'd take this chance
To lie down for a rest.

2.   Suddenly the wind got up
It blew and blew and blew.
The friends of Jesus all got scared
And wondered what to do.

The boat it tossed and turned about,
There was no time to think;
The water started rushing in,
The boat began to sink.

3.   Then they woke up Jesus
They thought they might all drown;
Jesus shouted out "BE STILL",
At once the wind died down.

Then Jesus gave his friends this pledge
That still today is true;
That if you always trust in God,
He'll always care for you.

OVERHEAD WORDS FOR DAVID AND GOLIATH (17)

1.   Young David was a shepherd boy,
   Lived on his father's farm.
   He had to fight off grizzly bears
   To save his sheep from harm.

   He taught himself to play the harp,
   He practised every day
   King Saul was told how good he was,
   So asked to hear him play.

2.   Now things were getting dangerous
   For all the Israelites;
   Their neighbours who were Philistines
   Were spoiling for a fight.

   They had a massive army,
   Goliath was in charge,
   Both strong and sly, and twelve foot high,
   Yes, he was very large.

3.   Goliath strutted up and down,
   He laughed, he jeered, he roared;
   He clattered in his armour plate,
   And swished his mighty sword.

   So who would fight this giant man?
   Saul wondered what to do.
   Then David boldly told the king:
   "I'll kill him off for you".

4. So David tried some armour on
Too big, it didn't fit.
He couldn't use his arms or legs,
Nor could he stand or sit.

But David had a better plan;
He'd fight him with his sling;
He knew that if he prayed to God
He reckoned he could win.

5. He swung his sling, a stone flew fast
Towards Goliath's head;
The giant screamed, crashed to the ground,
One hit – and he was dead.

The Philistines then fled away,
Saul's daughter David wed;
And when the king grew old and died,
Young David ruled instead.

OVERHEAD WORDS FOR
MR WISE AND MR FOOLISH (23)

1. Mr Wise he built a house,
He built it on a rock,
He dug, and dug, and worked so hard,
He worked right round the clock.

Then finally the job was done,
The house was built to last;
And when the wind and rain lashed down,
The house stood firm and fast.

2. Mr Foolish built his house,
Some sandy soil he found;
The house was very quickly built
On very shallow ground.

He hadn't lived there very long,
One night he was asleep;
A storm blew up and knocked it down,
It tumbled in a heap.

3. Down it fell because we know
His house was badly planned;
Mr Foolish should have known
His house would never stand.

The moral of this story,
It is easy now to tell;
So when you have a job to do (Pause)
(Slower)   Have faith and do it well.

30. GRANT US PEACE
(TO END AN EVENING SERVICE QUIETLY AND PRAYERFULLY)

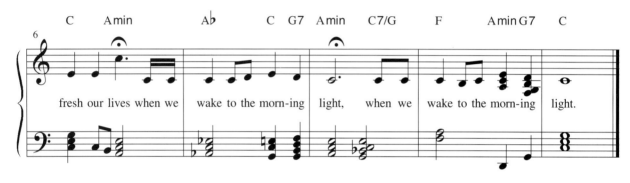

GRANT US PEACE

Grant us peace,
Grant us rest
And be with us tonight;
Renew our faith,
Refresh our lives
When we wake to the morning light
When we wake to the morning light.

John. Chapter 14. Verse 27.

'Peace I leave with you,
My peace I give you.
I do not give to you as the world gives.
Do not let your hearts be troubled and
do not be afraid.'
